MAN CLOWN DAYS DONE

Your Guide to Being A Boss Chick

JOVIAN MARKLAND

ISBN Number: 978-0-578-73126-1

Power Of Purpose Publishing
3355 Lenox Rd
Atlanta, Ga 30326
Www.PopPublishing.com
Www.LoveAndLiveYourMessage.com

CONTENTS

ACKNOWLEDGEMENT

If I should begin to individually thank everyone who influenced me to become the man I am today I would run out of pages. However, I must extend my sincere gratitude to God the almighty for the strength and guidance In life; he is the real MVP. I also must say thanks to my mom who raised me to become the man I am today, as she instilled values and morals that have carved me to the Markie you see today. I also would like to thank all of my elders in my family and community as their life long lessons are still of paramount importance in my life. Special thanks to all of my mentors who have mentored me, some have done so without even knowing me or meeting me ; I just look at their life story and testimony and have learned so much.

My beautiful island Jamaica has also played an important role in building me mentally, especially when I look at the injustice women go through daily. It pushes me to fight more for them; encouraging them and showing them that they deserve better treatment from men as they are becoming more successful than men as time progresses. I would also like to thank my students, thank you for the love, the

1

inspiration and sincerity you show to me; it truly helps me as I help you to school life.

BIG UP UNU SELF!

Introduction

I remember driving home one evening with one of my best friends as she sat in the passenger side of the vehicle venting her frustrations about her relationship to me. She went on about how she was unhappy with the fact that she was putting so much into her relationship and felt unappreciated. She continued to express her unhappiness about the relationship and how her partner had too much going on in his life, which seeped into her own life and made the relationship toxic and miserable. In addition, she had to work overtime to take care of him and the baby because he lost his job. Like the typical Markie, I tried to be the friend and offer words of encouragement while expressing my sincere thoughts about the situation. As you know, I had to keep it a hundred with her and told her it was just too much for her. Few minutes into our conversation, he called her phone and went off. I mean he was being disrespectful, rude, and ungrateful.

Of course, I tried to keep my mouth shut with every fiber of my being but that didn't last long. After she hung up, I exploded and that's how the world was introduced to me from the viral "Man Clown Days Done" video. I have always believed that women are some of God's most beautiful creations and deserve special care. It's no surprise that all of my closest friends are female. I watched my mom's struggle as a woman, single mother, survivor, and a father, all in one. I admired how she was able to wear all caps with strength, perseverance, and grace. Women are stronger than they think, they face so many of life's challenges in comparison to their male counterparts.

Thank you for using your hard-earned money to purchase my book; this indicates you are ready for a new phase of your life and ready to improve in all areas. As such, I write this book to inspire women and to remind them that they were made with special care, so anything or anyone in your life that does not make you feel this special should be eliminated. I write this book for women who can't find the beauty within themselves; for women struggling with self-acceptance; for those who feel like they can't find their way to achieving their dreams in life; and, most importantly, for women who have certain things in life holding them back from greatness. I will show you how to get back on track and take control of your destiny. I want to challenge you to start envisioning the life you want; manifest it and work towards it.

We all need love but sometimes, I feel like some women seek love at the expense of their happiness which is backwards to me. Signing up for love and a relationship should not look like you signed up for a circus for these lame men to treat you like a certified clown. Good girl, it's time to take off that big red nose and take up your crown. You deserve to be treated like a queen only if you act like one and believe you're one, and this is the problem. Ladies often don't see the queen in themselves so they take off their crown and put it aside to accept peasant treatment. It stops today! Man clown days done, we putting these lame men on punishment! I dare you to tell them 'hands on the wall' 'fingers on their lips'. Lock your shop, close your legs, and open your brains. You are a walking trophy, anybody who gets you should work for this reward. You have the definition of success all over you and between your legs. Start believing in your purpose and carry yourself like a queen. I'll be showing you how to do a 360 change in your life; from a basic bitch to a boss ass bitch. They call me the teacher and I'm ready to school you about life and have you graduate with flying colors. Class is in session. How it guh?

YOU'RE A WALKING TROPHY

Women are one of God's most beautiful creations. For the simple fact that you are brought on earth to continue the generation and serve as nurturers; speaks volume of the value you hold as a woman. As such, I want you to remember that in your natural state you are a walking trophy. You are always the prize possession in the relationship or your daily life. Everything about you makes you unique and no one can take that away from you. This is something you have to believe in order to live it. You can't believe you are basic and expect to look in the mirror and see a bad ass bitch! This is why I want you to love and appreciate every flaw, and if you can't accept anything you don't like, change it. Sis, life is too short to be a basic bitch. How it guh? Remember who made you; God makes no mistake so start to embrace your beauty because you were not made in China, you were heaven sent. If you know me, you would know I love myself a little too much and that's fine. When I look in the mirror, I see a bad ass bitch with the glimity glamity body set good "like ice inna freezer" and skin chrome like rims. And that's why when I enter the room, I may come off arrogant but it's confidence; I just happen to know that I'm that bitch so I act like it. So tell me, when you look in the mirror who do you see?

I have seen some of the most beautiful women walk around with the lowest self-esteem and it cripples every aspect of their lives as they rely on a man to make them feel pretty. This only makes them hurt more as these same men cause them so much pain. I know social media has made a lot of you ladies start to question your beauty. Trust and believe that I've met a lot of so-called social media bad bitches and they don't look like 20,000 likes in person. Stop looking at other women and comparing your beauty to theirs. Your gifts and beauty will never be the same as another woman's. Your beauty is unique and that's all you need to remember. Ain't a bitch like you and she can't do what you do, own that shit!

Before I go further, I want to know how much you value yourself. I told you that you are a walking trophy and I want to see if you see yourself as gold, silver, or bronze. Do the walking trophy exercise to give yourself an idea of where your self-esteem level is.

Walking trophy test

Look in the mirror and take a note of your physical attributes. On the left, list out everything you like about yourself and on the right list all the things you don't like.

I Love all of This!

I like my	I don't like my .....
1 smile	1
2 my teeth	2
3 texture of	3
4 my hair	4
5 ~~#~~ Aches scars	5
6 wrinkles	6
7 tummy	7
8 thickness	8
9 Fat ASS	9
10 nose	10

For everything you like about yourself continue to embrace them and for all the things you don't like let's start working on that.
If they can be fixed set some goals and start working on them. For the things you can't change, Start to mentally accept them as your unique beauty.

Appreciate your beauty and maximize on it. So if you want a bigger ass work on it; if you want better skin, change your skincare routine; if your hair won't grow, lay that lace front; if you hate the weight you see on the scale, trade fried chicken for a cucumber; and if you think you need a tighter vagina, sis grab a yoni stick, and if you want edges, mind your business. There are many ways to maximize your beauty. It's sometimes hard to accept your beauty when you were never told 'you are beautiful' especially while growing up or when you are a victim of verbal abuse by people who are supposed to call you beautiful and appreciate it. The truth is, you don't need anyone's approval, find your beauty within.

You have to fake it until you make it. Get up every day and tell yourself you are the prettiest girl in the world. Act like it, talk like it, dress like it, and demand to be treated as such. Eventually you will start to believe it and subconsciously, you will be that bitch. If you don't like anything about yourself and can't change it, embrace it. The truth is, we all have things about us that we don't like but once we start seeing beauty from within, we will embrace our flaws. In addition, ladies if you want to do a little work on your body to boost your confidence, go for it. Life is too short to walk around with low self-esteem. So, if a 360 lipo breast augmentation or butt lift is gonna boost your ego, go for it! Just as long as you're doing it for yourself and not for any one's approval. Don't let no one discourage you!

They often say beauty is in the eye of the beholder and this is why so many women look to a man for validation and this is where you go wrong. Truth be told, a lot of men don't know what true beauty is. They are attracted to a big ass, big boobs, fake hair and a face covered in makeup. This is why most men cannot appreciate true beauty in women and won't treat you like the queen you are. Beauty comes from within you! Once you believe this, you will exude it and it will show for people to appreciate. Start waking up every day to work on yourself. If you're overweight and have weight issues, start changing your diet, work out with a friend daily, stay motivated, and lose that weight. A lot of your confidence is lost in your belly and covered in fat and it starts with skipping a visit to KFC and taking a quick run in the park instead. As women, there is so much you can do to enhance your beauty like doing the right hairstyle, wearing the right makeup, and wearing the right clothes so you don't sit around in shame and insecurities. Change it and work it because you're a bad ass bitch in every way; you are walking with the definition of success in your brain and between your legs. Sweetheart, you are that bitch! So wake up every morning and affirm to yourself that you are a true bad bitch.

I challenge u to get up every morning and look in the mirror and do your daily affirmations.

I am a gold mine

I am beautiful strong and bold

I am the baddest bitch

This vagina will give me wealth

I will attract all good thing in my life

Protect me from all broke pocket men

I will attract healthy wealthy men

Always remember that the best asset a woman can walk with is her vagina and confidence; with them two you shall never fail. Your vagina has so much power beyond your imagination; she can birth a child and birth riches if you use her well. She never gets tired or will never expire. That's a gold mine, stop treating her like a bronze medal. Give her to men who can honor it and spend on it for the right value. Confidence should be your best secret weapon; I have seen some of the worse-shaped girls wear the most naked outfits and walk with their heads high and chest up because they are "goodaz" and they believe in themselves. Hun..... that's confidence. Do not care what people think about you, always remember you are the prettiest girl in the world. This is why a basic bitch will take these bad bitches men because they know they got it like that. You may be flawed in the eyes of someone else but once your confidence level is high, you will always feel like Beyoncé when you walk in the room. Another thing is don't mistake arrogance for confidence. A lot of women have all the right reasons to be confident but are afraid to show it because they fear what people will think. Fuck that! Bitch if you got it flaunt it and let them know you are beautiful, shaped nice, and you ain't afraid to show it. God gave it to you so embrace it. And when a man tells you you're beautiful say "THANK YOU I KNOW" just so he knows that you know your worth and love yourself already.

The worst thing I have ever seen women do is rely on men to make them feel pretty. I know sometimes your parents never told you that you're pretty, or due to past abusive relationships or traumatic experiences you lost confidence and felt ugly. This is something you must fix yourself as a woman and never rely on men to make you feel pretty. That would be the most crippling thing you can do because the moment he stops loving you, the moment he starts mistreating you, the moment he starts cheating on you or the moment he leaves you, you will start feeling ugly. And that's why most women lose confidence after a breakup because their man who was their cheerleader is no longer cheering on the sidelines. Men should complement you, not complete you so that when you are no longer with a man, you won't feel empty because he was your everything. Your partner should be the other half not your all. Start evaluating yourself and let's work on the areas you need help with that will boost your self-confidence. You need to be in love with yourself. No one will love you like you love yourself and this will affect how you see yourself, as well as how you allow people in your life to treat you. Self-love and confidence is a mental representation of how you see yourself, so it is very important to start seeing yourself as that beautiful queen. Once you love yourself, you will never accept certain things because you know your worth. I want you to see yourself as a true goddess from birth, so I created a chart below to help you with this.

"The goodaz" evaluation

Please rate each statement from 0 to 10 with 0 meaning you don't believe the statement at all and 10 means you completely believe the statement.

Evaluation statement

Ratings 0 to 10

1. I respect myself as a woman   _____
2. I love myself as I am   _____
3. I don't compare myself to other women   _____
4. I am happy to be myself   _____
5. I am proud of my accomplishments in life   _____
6. I don't regret the mistakes I made   _____
7. I love taking chances and trying new things   _____
8. I can handle criticism good or bad   _____
9. I love my body and embrace my flaws   _____
10. I focus more on my success than my failures   _____

Total score: _____

If your overall rating for your self-esteem is below 65 you need to do some work. You need to do some mental self-affirming work on these areas and start changing that.

Make of list of all these statements that are below a 6 and this will be your challenge to do whatever it takes to bring those up to atleast an 8.

1. _____   5. _____

2. _____   6. _____

3. _____   7. _____

4. _____   8. _____

Boss Bitch not a Bum Bitch

IN ORDER TO LOVE SOMEONE YOU MUST LOVE YOURSELF FIRST. In order to invest in a man, you must invest in yourself first, and in order to take care of anyone else, you must take care of yourself first. The worst thing I see women do is date a man that she has to take care of to the point where he looks better than her. Sis, that's no longer your man, that's your son. Some men are quick to ask women what they bring to the table and most times, you women are the entire table and chairs. Anyway, I think it's an important question both partners should ask each other because we must know the intentions and direction our spouses are looking for. However, in recent times, a lot of women are becoming independent and outshine the men's pocket. These women work hard and long hours, go to school, and find time to take care of their family and; in the midst of it all, still turn around and take care of a grown ass man. Money never equates to love so I don't know why women think taking care of a man will have him love her. That's just you getting him together to go cheat on you with some raggedy bum bitch, hurt your feelings, stress you out and the list goes on. This is why I

"raggedy" Ha Ha!

encourage women to work on their career and build success so they can attract successful men. You attract what you are; therefore a boss bitch will attract a boss man. Start working on yourself and manifest your counterpart but don't sit around broke, waiting for a man to save you.

Start investing in your career instead of spending so much time being pretty, alone. Looks fade away and this is why a lot of women stay fly but are bums in designer clothes. Ladies should be independent, not dependent. Your whole source of income should not be dependent on a man. Truth be told, if that's the case some women will forever be broke because they can't even keep a man. You should start bossing up and own businesses, start chasing your own dream, and make your own money so any man that comes into your life will add to your wealth. Therefore, when men approach you with certain material things, you won't be fooled into thinking love can be bought. However, you're still supposed to take their money. Start working on the life you want instead of thinking every man you meet is the guy to give you the dream life. Most of these men don't have a dream or sense of direction and if you depend on them to lead you, sweetheart you are on your way to the psychiatric ward; because the only thing some of them bring to the table is stress and headache.

Hold back on the Brazilian hair, hold back on the designers, close your legs and put that money in an online business. If there is a time to boss up, that time is now. It's so easy to gain financial wealth especially with social media but most of you use it to post naked pictures and argue with your so-called haters. Use your followers to make money not to gain hate. The same social media where a lot of you spend most of your time is making people millions daily; you can take advantage of this too. Take a break from social media and come back with an online business. You can start selling the same things that you spend most of your money on as other women out there also have the same spending habits. You can sell hair, clothes, beauty supplies, and the list goes on. Women just like you are making millions daily doing this. It's time to boss up, it's time to level up, no more excuses as life is passing you by. Starting a business online can be as easy as taking somebody's man. Think about what you want, forgetting about the obstacles and going for it just like how a lot of women ignore a man's wife and find their way in these relationships. Think of a product you want to sell and start thinking about how you can sell it and package it better than the competitors. Start working on getting the money to start this business which should not be hard. As I told you before, you are walking with a goldmine in your brain and between your legs. In fact, if you are smart, you should have a savings account. Go in the savings and instead of having the money sitting there with no interest, take a risk and start a business. If you can, ask a man for some money; either the one you're sleeping with or the one who is trying to get your attention. Nothing is free, not even your attention. Just let him know that giving you money is the best way to get it. Here is a simple chart below that breaks down the easy steps you can follow to start a booming online business.

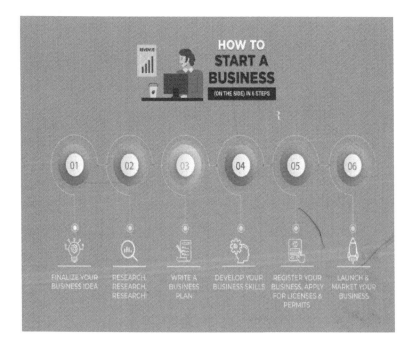

Stop thinking a man is coming to save you and this is what a lot of women do. They sit around and wait on a man to give them a breakthrough but instead he breaks their heart, their back, and their neck. Start bossing up on your own so when certain guys approach you, he understands he ain't messing with no average bitch so he knows he has to get his shit together. Sell some of your bags and get in your bag. Style and fashion fades with the season but a good education will never. Send yourself to school to invest in a degree, invest in a solid career that can bring you financial freedom. If your excuse is finances, there are so many ways around that. For some of you, your tuition fees are right in your closets. Sell some of those expensive bags, shoes, clothes, and jewelry, and use the money to invest in building a brand, a career, and a future.

Stop trying to compete with chicks around you, half of them are broke and only doing it for the 'gram'. Be your own competitor and invest in yourself; set your own goals and achieve them. A lot of the girls you're trying to keep up with are boosters who steal clothes. You can't keep up with bums in designer pieces, that's a losing battle. Underneath some of these so-called bad bitches that you look up to are bad reputations and sad stories. Stay in your own lane and work on you. Men know when women are fully dependent on them and this is why they treat some women like shit because he knows you want that money. So, he treats you bad knowing you will do anything for the money, and you will not go nowhere. However, when you have your shit together, you don't have to sit and endure certain disrespect because you already know a better life and you can provide that life for yourself without him. You may not have an education and can't see yourself going back to school but there are so many ways to earn a living these days. A lot of females are very talented and can turn these gifts into a fortune. As I said before:

If you can do nails, you're a nail tech

If you can do hair, you're a hairstylist

If you can do lashes, you're a lash tech

If you can sew clothes, you're a seamstress

If you can boost clothes, open your boutique

If you can give good head, you're a headist

If you can take good nude pix, join Onlyfan

Women are blessed with many talents and skills. Use them wisely and make a fortune but don't sit around waiting for a man to save you. Some of these men are lost themselves. A lot of men are dealing with mental issues that they will never talk about because they think it will soften their masculinity. This is why a lot of them won't show you true love. It's very important that you treat yourself as a woman, love yourself, worship yourself so when a man comes around, he understands that this is now his job and you would do the same for him. However, don't expect from a man what you can't do for yourself or don't even know how to do.

Always understand the importance of assets over hype. The glitz and glam will all fade away. One day Doctor Miami won't be able to do anything for you, clothes will no longer sit perfectly on your body, makeup wont hide the bags under your eyes, and long colorful extensions on your head will make you look like a clown (even though some of you do look like a perfect clown already). The only thing that will matter is having a good life that you have made for yourself so we should never get sidetracked, focusing on the wrong things because life goes by fast. This is the reason why you will find some of these dancehall veterans in parties even when they are old, searching for something they can't find. Let's be real, there is more to life than partying, drinking and taking pictures. All while trying to create an illusion of happiness. Why put so much energy to show up to an event where no one likes you? Why not show up on a beautiful island for a vacation to have a blast and create true memories of happiness.

Ladies self-care is the best care; get your hair and nails done all the time along with your facials. So when a man meets you, he meets you fully pampered and understands that if he is going to be with you, he is dealing with a badass bitch that should be maintained. Men love women that look good but truly appreciate a woman with beauty and a plan behind it. Looks are not everything because beauty can be bought in the Sephora store, having a career and a plan behind your beauty is the true definition of a bad bitch. Looks cannot hold that title by itself, if that's the case then hunny you're not a bad bitch, you're only doing bad.

Looking like success is very important but if you look like success and your life in reality is a failure, you create a fairytale life that does not exist. I've seen countless women walk around looking snatched, hair, makeup and nails on fleek, dressed in latest pieces, drive latest cars, and have no money in their bank account, own no true assets, have no real career or business, and think they are winning; sis you're Alice in Wonderland. Wake up. Walk in your purpose, actualize your true purpose, and live out your dreams. Believe in yourself and start somewhere. Success looks like a long road especially when you were not born with a gold spoon in your mouth but other women just like you who have way less than you did it. So what's your excuse?

Find a mentor who can teach you the way to a successful business or career path, read books instead of sitting around all day on social media and gossiping with friends on the phone. Reach out to successful women and ask for help instead of hating on them. Even ask some of the successful men you are sleeping with to help you because they are not even taking care of you. The least they can do is share some knowledge instead of only sharing empty dick.

I know you may not be where you want to be in life, I believe you can achieve anything you put your mind to. Stop comparing yourself to others, their chapter 6 may be your chapter one; just start your journey as I told you before, "take up the cross and follow Jesus". Stop trying to compare yourself to someone else, work on your own path to success and make yourself the complete package in order to meet a man that can complement you. A man should complement you and what you have going on. Some of you are looking for a savior because you're lost and in need of total help. In that case, sis you don't need a man, you need Jesus because you're looking for a miracle to turn your water into wine.

Let's start with getting rid of the bad bitch syndrome, because a lot of women call themselves a bad bitch but really have a lot of bad in their life

- Bad bank account
- Bad credit
- Bad self-esteem
- Bad relationship
- Bad career

Let's start aiming to be boss bitches who have a complete purpose in life and a level of success that we work towards. Sit for a moment and list out all areas of your life that you are not satisfied with and think about how you're going to change it. Create the life you want for yourself and work on it. Miss Independent is the best hashtag you can use. Don't sit around waiting on a prince charming to give you life, start your own journey and he will come along and join the movement. Be the main driving force in your destiny. Let's start with a vision board; go to the store, get some magazines and cut out images that represent your future business, future husband, future career, and future life. Put it in a spot in your house where you can see it every day and manifest to yourself "favors; cometh to me now". Yes sis, speak life over your vision board every day. Good life! Here is an example of my vision board.

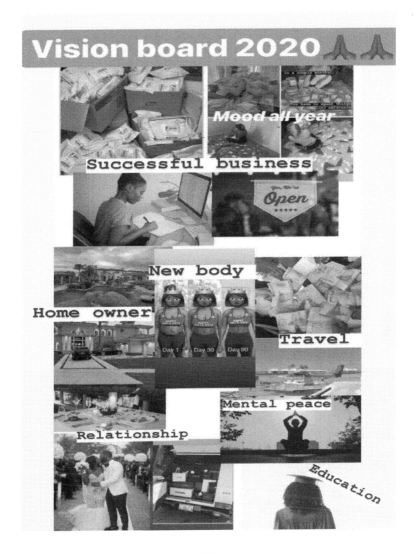

Be reminded that the vision board is no use without a plan and execution. A lot of women have in their IG bio CEO, boss lady, wifey, but in reality, those titles don't exist. A vision is nothing without action so if you already have a business, you constantly need to think bigger for it and plan for growth. If you don't have a business or the career you want, it's time to plan and start working towards it. Start reading books in your field of interest, start watching YouTube videos, reach out to some mentors for guidance, and expand your knowledge. Then sit and write down your business plan and as you execute each step, cross it out. This is the real competition you need in life, not trying to keep up with women who are doing better than you. Let your goals in life be your competition.

BAGGAGE OR BAE?

The best thing you can ever give a man is your time and sacrifice, something you will never get back when wasted in a relationship. I've seen countless women waste their best years in relationships that were nothing but toxic. Then spend their future upset and bitter when they think of how foolish they were. It's like you're the main character on stage in the circus. You try to put on a show acting like you have the best relationship or you have relationship goals but to us, you're a man clown with the biggest red nose. The good news is by purchasing this book, you are about to walk out of the circus and walk into growth and happiness because MAN CLOWN DAYS DONE!

Old people would say love is blind but I think a lot of you women pick up men trying to be "Xena the man hero". You have seen all the red flags and just think he is going to change one day or you are going to fix him. Sweetie, this is not fixer upper, molly build a man! Stop trying to change a grown man. You can't raise a man, he is already a grownass man set in his ways. So, if you're dating a dog and hoping he will change into a nice husband, that will never happen. If you're dating an abuser and expect him to treat you good, it won't happen. If you're dating a lying, cheating womanizer and expect the truth, dream on. As my grandmother would say, "stop wasting white powder on black bird". Men don't change, they adjust and then show their true colors.

Truth be told, a lot of men in some of our lives are baggage. They set us back from being ourselves and living in our purpose. In fact, a lot of men in our lives are actually cock blockers! Blocking you from the husband you have been praying for since you were a little girl. Let's be real, men will never be perfect but some of these men don't even deserve to smell the crotch of a woman. They don't add to your life, they stand in your way and just serve as straight up baggage.

Understand that if you're a queen, you deserve a king and nothing less. Don't get off your throne to date the help unless he is trying to sit on the throne as a king. Sadly, this is what a lot of women do. Lower their standards and date men who are not ready for them, start taking care of them, then try to turn him into something he is not, a real man. Before entering into something serious with a man today, you have to really sit and study him. Study the way he treats you, the way he protects you, the way he spends on you, the way he talks about you when you're not around. These are ways you can separate a fuck buddy from a partner. Yes that's right! Some men only serve the purpose of giving you some good sex when you want it and no relationship with him. Ain't nothing wrong with seeing a man that only blows your back out every now and then and you both understand that it's nothing personal, no strings attached; well, only string attached is dollar signs (no free fuck). This is better than dating a man for years only because you fell in love with the sex and became "dickmatized". I'm not saying we have a sex problem, we all have sexual needs and some of the best sex comes from broke men. Child I can tell y'all. They serve no other purpose in our lives but great sex. After that comes nothing and we need to not make sex the main deciding factor when choosing our partners.

Many women would say "Markie you will never find the perfect man" and that's absolutely true. However, you can definitely manifest someone who treats you right and adds value to you as a life partner. You have to look at relationships more seriously. Don't think you're just passing time, you are wasting time, and the time you waste dating someone who is not meant for you will only set you back if you don't get out fast enough. Granted, some relationships are mistakes meant to be made as it's a lesson to be learned to show you the type of men to not fall for; so when you make the same mistake over and over, you now become a certified man clown. It's not bad when you have a relationship that turned sour and you get to experience hurt and disappointment because you get to understand what not to tolerate in your next relationship. In all fact, you have to lose sometimes in order to win.

If you're with a man for over a year, it is time to get things into perspective. Start asking these men, "What plans do you have for me? What can you do for me? What are our visions? What's our goal?" It is imperative we ask these questions to understand their mindset as it will completely make you realize where the relationship is going. Some men do add value to your life while dating them, however, some are straight up baggage holding you back from your purpose.

Imagine dating a man for a couple of years and all you have to show is pictures; that is if he even showed his face in them. In fact, I'm a firm believer in not broadcasting or posting pictures of men you're dating who are not securing you a future or the bag. This is the worst mistake you can make as a woman. In the social media world we exist in today; your future husband may be following you for months and just doesn't have the courage to slide in your DM. Be careful what you post and who you post. A lot of women are posting some worthless men who they are temporarily dating with captions like "hanging with bae". Sis that's not bae, that's your carryon baggage, hang him up! He is slowly blocking you from receiving your blessing; the man you dream of, the man specially handcrafted by God for you. Unless he proves to you he is the one, someone you can grow and build with, someone who will protect and provide for you, someone who you can count on without a shadow of a doubt, DON'T POST HIM! NO FREE PROMOTION because that's exactly what you are doing, promoting him for other thirsty bitches to slide in his DM while blocking a real husband from popping up in your DM. We only promote real men who are worth that kind of praise. PERIOD!

Ladies it's 2020, don't waste no time with these men, let them know straight up you are looking for a future. Not another sad song to sing. You want a man with goals and aspirations, a man who can help you create the future you want. Your time is precious and so is your vagina, so if you choose to spend some on him, it should yield rewards not just heartache, stress, and unnecessary increase in vagina mileage. When you are in a relationship, you and your partner should be looking at a house, a family, a business, travel the world, and share happy moments. It can't be just dry sex. Truth be told, half of them don't even make you orgasm, so you can definitely do without them. Besides, you can get a fuck buddy or a sex toy which I'm sure most of you have already since most men can't even make a bitch buss a nut. There are some guys that came with some other luggage that you slowly gotta deal with in the relationship that you never saw coming, as they are good at putting out their best side for the first few months. Granted, men won't be perfect and they all have a flaw to deal with. However, if they are not trying to work on themselves to better themselves, this is a red flag.

At this point, you are finding yourself in a relationship that is turning into a sinking ship. Some partners can be insecure and jealous,this seems cute at first as you think your pussy is so good he just can't keep his eyes off you, but it can lead to death. I can tell you countless stories of jealous partners that ended up hurting their partners, so take this as a red flag because sooner or later, it will be a big thing in the relationship. You won't be able to go to certain places with friends and have the fun you want as his jealous ways won't allow it. Then you become a prisoner as he does not trust you around no one but himself so he wants to make sure you're always around him alone. This is not ok and it's baggage; a man should never lock you off from the world and most of the times, they will say they are jealous because they love you but that's not an excuse. If he loves you, he would be happy to see you live free. A lot of them are only jealous because they are doing something wrong and they are playing reverse psychology on you; their own demons are haunting them and they take it out on you. As a woman you should be free, happy, and live life like it's golden.

Know the difference between a controlling man and a man who takes control. I have a friend who is so controlled by her man it is a shame. I call her Toshiba remote as he literally controls her entire life to the point where her life is so miserable. I mean she can't do nothing without his consent, and I asked her, 'Why do you stay?' It's so sad when an adult is controlled by someone who is supposed to love them and see them happy. I just don't understand. Ladies, it is never ok to be controlled by a man, they have mental issues deep rooted within them and need to be taken care of. Another major baggage in relationships that needs to be pointed out is men who don't trust you.

I often ask, "Why date someone you don't trust?" I feel like that's a lot of work to balance. Love is pure and true. To be in love with someone means completely believing in them and trusting them so I can't understand why men say they are in love with women yet still don't trust them. This is one of the most toxic traits a man can have as it affects every aspect of the relationship. He will never believe anything you say. He will do any and everything to keep you under his wings because he doesn't trust you enough. Lack of trust from men, most times, becomes obsessive and abusive. Men understand their dominance over women and use it to their advantage, which is why they love when women are submissive and fearful of them. Don't think for a second this is ok. If you're with a man, you should feel like you have a voice. Some men love when you act like dummies so they can stroke their ego. Not on my watch! You should have a voice, you should have a life outside of your relationship. Men should trust you enough to let you go out with friends and be happy. If you are experiencing this level of control and lack of love from your spouse, well sis, you need a reality check and that reality check might be a coffin like many beautiful women end up in while dating controlling men; so act fast and demand a change.

Let's not forget the men who are abusive, which is the worst trait a man can have. Your body is a work of art, it is your sanctuary. The only damage you want is pleasurable sexual damage to the vagina as it repairs itself. Men should never beat on women PERIOD. A lot of us grow up seeing this kind of behavior so it seems normal, yet it's disgusting pig behavior. A man should worship your body not destroy it. Most men have mental issues and take it out on women but I say, if a man beats you once, pack your shit and leave. But if you sit and take it for the second time, that's your invite to constant abuse. Never say never, so if it happens once, which it should not, take it as a big red flag. Actually it should be a stop light, a deal breaker even if he is giving you the world because you can end up losing your life one day. It ain't worth it, no form of physical abuse is right, especially from your man. The female body is made like a work of art, not a boxing bag.

Then there are those men who come with unnecessary drama in your life like side chicks disrespecting you, baby mother drama, cheating drama, and the list goes on. Sis, let me make it clear. According to Professor Markie, no matter how pretty you are, sexy you are, rich you are, tight you are; nothing exempts you from being cheated on. That's not a surprise; it's the level of respect he does it with. We all have a past; a part of his past may be a baby mother but one thing you should never stand around and allow is for him to think for a second it's okay to disrespect you. Let's be real "wife a wife, mate a mate". She should always know her place and he should make sure this never happens. If you find yourself in this kind of drama and as a man he cannot control this, he needs to be checked. Respect is of utmost importance and he needs to man up and take care of this mess. Sit on your throne and be the queen you are and never come off to throw tomatoes with ex-girlfriends; that's his job as you never dated her; he did.

Now I know I mentioned a few traits men could have that makes them baggage, but I think the worse baggage a man could ever come with is being broke. I strongly believe a man with no money don't deserve vagina. As the bible says, "A man that don't work don't deserve to eat" and that includes the eating of your vagina. Men should be providers in the house not dependents. God made Adam first, as he knew the task men had on earth. So, even if you make more money than him, that's no excuse to take care of him. You're a FEE-MALE. You are a male that comes with a fee and if he can't pay the fee, then he needs to be with a male, which is himself. That should be one of his main priorities; to take care of his family. As I mentioned earlier, you should be able to provide for yourself, and if you are in a relationship, your man should know the part he plays in the house; a provider not a dependent. Nothing good in life is free,including your time, love, and vagina.

Be careful of men who are also verbally abusive. Sometimes words cut deeper than knives, hence why some women lose their entire self-esteem after dealing with some men. As a man, it is a part of his job to make you feel like the prettiest girl in the world even though you should already know and believe this as a woman. He must express to you how much he loves you, how much he cares, and how much you make him a better man. Granted everyday won't be all fine and dandy but certain words should not come out of a man's mouth to his woman. Words are powerful and if a man talks down to you as a woman, your subconscious will slowly start to believe it and you will start acting like it. There are so many women who are verbally abused by men and become so insecure and vulnerable as it plays on the mind. If you're a victim of this kind of behavior, seek help asap and get back your confidence, build up your ego, and start believing in your worth as a woman.

Somewhere along the line some women decide to change the narrative and take care of men. Those are the main acts in the circus. Now, I'm not saying you cannot help your man get his life together and put him on the right track to success; but don't sit there and play man hero or give charity, which is exactly what some women do. They take care of men fully. They work long hours just to take care of a man and themselves, while he sits around watching them work themselves to death. That's never a good look; women come with certain expenses by just being women, the hair, nail, shopping, dinners, vacations; these are basics that come with being his girlfriend. Since you should be able to do this for yourself, if you have a man, what makes him think he should not do it for you as well? Don't mistake this for him going above and beyond for you; this just comes as part of being a man. In addition, if he decides to take you to a nice restaurant, pay the bills in the house, or book you a special vacation, this is an addition to what he should be doing. I call it a tip to the bill; you deserve more. Even if you work for your own money, it should be a part of his agenda to take care of his woman's basic financial needs. If you find yourself taking care of a man, that's a form of baggage that is not a good characteristic in your future husband. Cut it out now and have this conversation with him. Let him know you can't do his job for him as you have yours as his woman already. Now, let's sit for a moment and evaluate your relationship. Make a list of the good traits in your partner and the bad traits. If the good outweigh the bad, way to go! "Ye gyal yuh bingo". However, if the bad outweighs the good that may be an overweight baggage that should be left at the airport. Here is a chart below where we can separate the good and bad qualities and figure out if we are overweighing ourselves with unnecessary baggage.

Baggage or bae

Make a list of the good and bad qualities below. These qualities should be the most prominent in the relationship.

Good qualities	Bad qualities
1	1
2	2
3	3
4	4
5	5
6	6
7	7
8	8
9	9
10	10

Lose to Win Again

As a woman; you would often find yourself in a position where you question certain aspects of your life. You start to evaluate and analyze, then ask yourself, "What can you do for me?" Well in this chapter, I want you to pose this question to yourself, your friends, and your current partner if you have one. Sis life is short, we have no room for baggage in our life that yields no reward or progress and sometimes we can be the biggest baggage in our own life. We have certain habits and traits that set us back. We are never perfect but we can at least strive for a better version of ourselves daily.

A lot of women have terrible trust issues, and this has affected them in so many aspects of their lives, especially in relationships. You may have been through a very traumatic experience in your life especially when you were a minor; this may include rape, molestation, betrayal, physical abuse, and the list goes on. Now as a young woman this will definitely affect you personally, I'm here to tell you that you have to forgive and flourish. Now I know you may say, "Markie you don't know what I've been through and how painful it was" but I can definitely tell you that someone has been through way worse than you and they never allowed their past to determine their future. That's exactly what you do when you don't forget about the past and try to make the best out of your future.

I had a close friend who was molested by her own father for years; just imagine having your virginity taken by someone who is supposed to protect you in life? Just imagine how she felt everyday having to live with that reality all of her life. Well it definitely affected her, she was always angry, always felt like less of a woman, so she became promiscuous. She never felt pretty, so she never trusted anyone in her life. This is too much hate and anger to walk around with I would think. So, one day after breaking down to me and explaining what happened and why she acts the way that she does, I was really taken back and felt really bad for her. Then I asked about her dad's whereabouts and she told me he died. So I said to her, "Why are you mad at someone who is dead? Why bother making your life miserable over someone who is not even alive?" I told her forgiving him and healing herself would be the best thing she could ever do.

Ladies, I would never take away your past experience but I can definitely tell you that you have to forgive in order to attract good in your life. Life throws us all sorts of struggles but that's what makes our story special. You may have felt like you had the worst experience in your past but it's never a failure; it's always a lesson learned and you have to take it and forget about it in order to be a kickass survivor. Stop making your past affect your future. This is why some of you women can't even love and trust your current man, because you were once dating a piece of shit who literally made your life a living hell. Now that God has sent you a blessing, you can't even love him as you are supposed to because you're still mad and angry at your ex. Baby girl, stop holding on to things in life that make you a bitter person, forgive but never forget and you can always use that past experience to conquer future struggles in life. Forgive your mom who hurt you, forgive that man that abused you and used you to the ground, forgive anyone that caused you any pain. It can start with a simple phone call to the person and just simply saying 'I'm forgiving you for all the pain you have caused me". Forgive them, not to make them feel better but to make you feel better and have a better chance of living life to the fullest. Holding on to pain only blocks your blessings and makes you bitter. Stop holding grudges with people; this makes you even uglier as your insides become packed with hate and anger over things you hold on to. Have you ever seen someone who is just very bad-minded and evil, then on the outside they look even uglier? That's what hate does. Lose these old habits and watch your life get better, see how you can achieve mental peace, and attract all good things into your life.

Start looking at your current friends and ask the question "friend or frenemy?" Our closest friend may be our worst enemy. If God was like man and could reveal the evil thoughts that some of your so-called friends have for you, I promise you would not look at them the same. I am not insinuating that all friends are not genuine, however, not all that glitters is gold and not all best friends have your best interests at heart. This is why I want you to sit and go through your circle and ask them, "What can you do for me?". As women, it's very natural for us to have a posse or crew of friends as most of us feel the need for a sense of fellowship in our lives. Women typically find comfort in each other as we share common interests and similar life experiences, yet you have to be careful.

My grandmother once said, "Show me your company and I'll tell you who you are." Your friends will be the main factor holding you back from living in your purpose, stop you from getting the man of your dreams, stop you from achieving your goal, and the list goes on. You have to be extremely careful of the friends you keep as some of them only want to get clout off your name. Bitches are thirsty, they will friend you just to get clout off your name, just to be a part of the hot gyal crew and build a name off you. They will be around you all day and mean you no good. If you want to know a real friend, watch and see how they act when you have an argument or malice. The first thing some of them will do is expose your secrets! That's the most deadly friend you can have. They will sit in your face and chat behind your back, take your man, be friends with your enemy, and even go as far as kill you for the life you live.

You cannot be friends with somebody that wants your life and this is why a lot of women always fall out. As soon as you start having success and happiness, they want it instead of aspiring to be like you and be happy for you. You can't be friends with someone that wants your man, wants your career, wants your style, wants your clout, wants your money, or just wants your everything. They should be inspired by you because real friends are supposed to inspire each other to shine and succeed but not to want their friend's success. You should also understand that trust is a big aspect of a real friendship; if you can't leave your friend around your man, that's not a friend. If you can't trust your friend with your secrets, that's not a friend. If you can't find inspiration and motivation through your friend, that's not a friend. And if you can't depend on your friend when in need, that's nowhere near a friend.

Friends should want to see each other win and find love and happiness, not envy or tear each other down. Friends are meant to inspire you to be the best version of yourself and this is why some girls are stagnant as their friends are some bum bitches with no real goals other than IG goals; so they become a bum bitch too. I never really see a lawyer or doctor hanging with janitors. So show me your company and I will tell you who you are. If you want to win, hang with winners but some of us are calling some swear losers who may be exuding generational curses on you that may be blocking your blessings; 'bestie'. This bum bitch energy is all you have in your life as you spend so much time with your friends and share their energy. This is why you can't get the man you want because they tell you he is too good for you. This is why you can't get the business that you want because every time you tell them your plans, their bum ass talks you out of it. This is why you won't go back to school because you allow them to tell you that fucking with a scammer and being a bad bitch will be better than getting an education and the career you want. Another major blockage in your life can be your significant other in your life.

There are some good men out there, a lot of women complain that they can't find a good man but you may be surprised at how many good men you turn down because he is not your type. The irony is a lot of good men are around you waiting to enter your life; you just won't give them a chance. We are stuck on focusing on Mr. Wrong. Man clown days done! Do not sit with no man that can't offer you anything in life but dick. If that's the case, sis go grab you a dildo or vibrator from my website (markyourpleasure.com). Truth be told, half of them give you a headache and no good head. Trust me sis, you're better off without them. It's time you really sit and start manifesting the right man in your life. List out the qualities you want in a man and start praying until he shows up. One of my cousins was with a broke ass bum who literally ruined her life. She was with him for over seven years and had nothing to show but stress and tears. I mean she was the leader of the man clown movement. By the grace of God and me cursing her all day she left him; found a good African man, got married, got her degree, got a great job and started her family, all in less than two years. When I tell you some men are curses, blocking you from your future husband. Don't settle!

Any man you have in your life should be able to provide for and protect you. This is a vital necessity in any relationship. There should be no reason for you to be with a man who can't provide for his family. So if you're with a man that can't offer financial security, sweetheart you're a pedophile, report to the nearest police station, that's not a man that's a boy! Not implying that men should shoulder all responsibilities; but he must understand his role as a man and never question it. Women are beautiful creatures that take pride in keeping up their feminine side so the hair, nails, shopping are basic rituals your man should KNOW you have to do and pay for it. It's way more expensive to be a woman; don't ever think for a second you should pay for all of this if you're with a man. This should be something he should gladly want to do for his woman, pamper her. So if a man will sit and look at a woman and tell her he won't do this, then that's not a real man.

Men should be able to run their households with the help of a woman, not sitting and watching a woman do it on her own. Remember, women are becoming more independent which doubles their work, women now work and do housework (if she doesn't have a maid), cooks and takes care of the family domestically. Now, do you think it's fair for a woman to do that plus provide for the family and the man? Ladies, you're not a gold digger but you have a value and a purpose in the relationship that must be met, no exception; if he can't meet you at least halfway, sis, no meet up at all.

A man in your life should make you feel like the prettiest girl in the world, even though this is something you should enter into your relationship already knowing. Remember you're a queen and you should be dating a king who shows you your worth; so he should never do anything to intentionally hurt you. However, a lot of women sit around with men who constantly have them crying. They hurt and disrespect you daily with no remorse. My question is, "Why do you stay?" Why go through this when you can drop that man and find a better man? Sis, as one man gone another man born, we have plenty fish in the sea. The problem is a lot of women are attracted to the bad guys who care zero about them and only care about themselves, so how do you expect to get the good guy out of a bad guy? I have seen women turn down successful men just to be with broke men. I have seen women stick around with abusive men while good men are begging her to show her a better life. I have seen even my own friends stick around with the biggest cheaters who do it with no respect for her while good men are waiting to marry her.

Moral of the story is, stop sitting around with these good for nothing men who have nothing good to offer you while your future husband is sitting around watching you waste time. Not saying that there is a perfect man but there are definitely good guys out there. If you are in a current relationship and you know it's not working out, stop sitting there hoping it works itself out. Start having this conversation with your man. Ask him, "Babe what can you do for me?" Tell him how you feel, tell him how you want to be treated, tell him what's affecting you in the relationship, tell him your dreams and aspirations, and ask him how he can work with you to achieve them. If he does not have a plan to meet you half way then sweet heart let him go! You can't fail. One gone, another is born right there, waiting for you!

Believe in your happiness; believe in your power as a wife to find a good husband. Stop limiting your potential with these men who can't handle a real woman, and a real queen. Walk away from it. You can't fail, success is in your mind and between your legs. You already have the definition of success in you. I promise, you got this! We all have a soul mate, stop blocking your blessings with these fuck boys! How it guh?

Starting over ain't the end. No more crying, no more sitting around questioning your worth. You are worth a good man, you are worth feeling loved, you are worth happiness, you are worth honesty, you are worth having a cheerleader in your life that cheers for you even when you fail. I am not implying that all men are no good, nor am I implying that all relationships are no good but if you find yourself in a stressful relationship that you know you are not happy with, let it go. However, if you believe there is hope in your current relationship, start working on it and fight for the change you want. It won't work itself; the time is now, start fixing what needs to be fixed. However, if you think you have tried enough and it's not going nowhere, sis Break up to glow up. Man clown days done!

Manufactured by Amazon.ca
Bolton, ON